T0045037

Ladders

Living in the DESERT

Communities We Live In

Prickly Plants

by Nathan W. James

There are places in the world where it hardly ever rains and water is scarce. They are called **deserts**. A desert gets little rain each year. Most deserts are quite hot. Even so, many things live there. One type of plant grows well in a desert—the **cactus**.

> This is the Sonoran Desert in Arizona. Many different types of cacti grow in this desert. Some have thick, straight trunks. Others are shaped like a barrel. Some have flat, leaflike pads. These pads can look like the wide end of a boat paddle.

If you've ever touched a cactus, you know it's not like other plants. It has a waxy coating that helps it hold water inside. Cacti (more than one cactus) are made up mostly of water. Many cacti have sharp needles on their stems instead of leaves. Needles protect a cactus from animals that might harm it. Animals don't want to be poked by the pointy needles. Some clever creatures have learned to avoid them to get to the water inside the cactus.

Thirsty desert animals sometimes scratch their way into a cactus to eat its watery insides. These animals carefully avoid the needles. Then they dig through the waxy coating. On a blazing hot desert day, they will work hard to enjoy a cool piece of cactus.

A Gila woodpecker hollows out a hole in a saguaro cactus. Inside, it makes its nest. Screech owls and other animals might move in after the woodpecker leaves.

As Tall As a House

Cacti provide desert animals with more than just food and water. There aren't many trees in deserts. Birds must find other places to build nests. Some birds, such as the Gila (HEE-luh) woodpecker, peck holes in cacti. A hole in a cactus is a perfect place for a woodpecker to nest.

Other birds live in saguaro (suh-WAH-ro) cacti. The saguaro is what most people think of when they think of a cactus. You've probably seen them in a cartoon. Saguaros only grow in the Sonoran Desert. That desert stretches from the western United States to Mexico. The saguaro is the tallest cactus in the United States. It can grow taller than a one-story house. It has bent "arms" that grow from a tall center stem.

A saguaro cactus usually begins to grow a branch out of its side when it's 50 to 70 years old. That may sound old, but it's young for a saguaro. These tall cacti can live to be 200 years old!

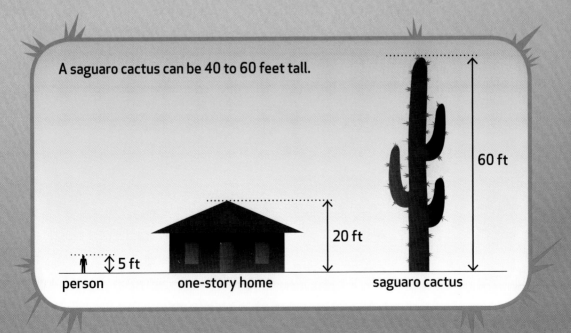

A saguaro cactus can be 40 to 60 feet tall.

5 ft — person

20 ft — one-story home

60 ft — saguaro cactus

Cactus for Lunch

The saguaro lives in only one desert. But the prickly pear cactus grows in deserts all over the world. Prickly pears are shorter than saguaro cacti. They grow to be seven feet tall, or a little taller than a grown man. The prickly pear cactus is another desert plant that makes a good home for small animals and birds. Its thick pads and needles protect birds' nests from enemies.

Prickly pear cacti make good lunches for humans—minus the needles, of course. People cook and eat prickly pear pads called *nopales* (no-PAH-layz). First, the cactus needles are removed from

Farmers pick nopales and bring them to markets.

the flat, leafy pads. Then the pads are grilled and served like a steak. They taste a little like green beans.

Prickly pear cacti get their name from their fruit. The fruit looks like a pear with small spines. When the fruit is ripe, it is bright red. It can be cut in half and eaten like a cantaloupe. Many people use the pears to make jams and jellies. They taste a little like watermelon bubble gum, and they turn your tongue red.

> Nopales salad

This woman is cleaning nopales pads at a market. She wears gloves to make sure she isn't pricked by the nopales' needles. The needles are small and hard to see.

Check In Why do cacti have a waxy coating and needles instead of leaves?

SANDY SETTLE

by Jennifer A. Smith

Hairy, Scary

A desert is a tough place to live. It can be very hot during the day and very cold at night. It gets little rain. But many animals live in the desert in spite of these rough conditions. Let's look at how these animals have **adapted** to living in the desert. How are their bodies designed to survive in this hot, dry place?

The tarantula (tuh-RAN-chuh-luh) is a very large, hairy spider. It lives in the deserts of the United States and Mexico. During the day, the tarantula sleeps in a **burrow**. That's a hole that is dug in the sand. Daytime is much hotter than nighttime in the desert. The tarantula avoids the heat by sleeping during the day. And because its burrow is underground, it stays cooler there.

The tarantula hunts for food at night, when temperatures drop. Like other spiders, the tarantula mainly eats insects. It does not spin a web, though. It catches its food by pouncing on it. Fortunately, the desert is full of bugs to snack on!

< Tarantulas know when other animals are near. They feel tiny motions through the ground and in the air.

The Horse of the Desert

Camels have been helping humans transport heavy loads through deserts for thousands of years. Most camels have one hump, but some have two. They are called Bactrian (BAK-tree-uhn) camels. They live in deserts in Asia. These deserts are very hot in summer and very cold in winter.

Many people think camels use their humps for storing water. Actually, camels store fat in their humps. Their bodies use that fat for energy when food is hard to find.

∨ These Bactrian camels are crossing a desert in China.

Camels have adapted to survive for a long time without food and water. This allows these animals to live in **arid**, or dry, climates. Bactrian camels can survive on the water they get from eating grasses that grow in the desert during the winter.

Like one-humped camels, Bactrian camels have nostrils that can shut tight. That keeps the blowing desert sand out of their noses. Bactrian camels grow a thick coat of hair to keep them warm in the cold desert winters. They shed their coats when summer comes, so they don't get too hot.

Bactrian camels have two rows of long eyelashes. The lashes protect their eyes from blowing sand.

Made for Desert Living

The kangaroo rat is a **rodent**. It lives in the arid deserts of the United States, Canada, and Mexico. A rodent is a small animal with big front teeth for chewing. Mice and squirrels are rodents. The kangaroo rat has adapted to desert living. Its large back feet help it hop and jump quickly through desert sand.

The kangaroo rat almost never drinks water! It gets the water it needs from eating the seeds of desert plants. That behavior helps it live in the desert.

∨ This kangaroo rat peeks from its burrow.

Like the tarantula, the kangaroo rat digs a burrow in the ground. The burrow protects the rodent from the heat of the desert. The kangaroo rat leaves its burrow at night to search for seeds. It gathers them in its cheeks. Then it brings the seeds back to the burrow where it stores them. If the desert gets too hot, or if a rainstorm comes, the kangaroo rat will have enough stored food to stay in its burrow for days.

Kangaroo rats have many predators, or animals that hunt them for food. But they have excellent hearing to help them stay safe. They listen carefully for animals, such as owls flying quietly overhead. Then they can escape into their burrows before it's too late.

‹ Kangaroo rats don't sweat. That means their bodies keep a lot of water.

A Desert Monster

The Gila (HEE-luh) monster isn't a monster. It's a big lizard. It lives in the deserts of the United States and Mexico. It can grow to be nearly two feet long, and it can weigh up to five pounds.

The Gila monster gets water from the food it eats. It eats the eggs of desert birds. It also eats small animals. Like a camel stores fat in its humps, the Gila monster stores fat in its tail. It can go months between meals, living off its stored fat.

Like the tarantula and kangaroo rat, the Gila monster lives in a burrow. It spends nearly all of its time there, away from the desert heat. Once in a while, it comes out to hunt or to warm itself in the sun.

Though Gila monsters have a poisonous bite, they only use it against threatening enemies. They really aren't dangerous to people.

A Gila monster's skin has orange, yellow, or pink patterns. The colors tell animals that the Gila monster is poisonous.

Check In Tell how one of the animals you read about has adapted to living in the desert.

Desert Pen Pals

by Nathan W. James

There are deserts all over the world. Some are hot, some are cold. But all of them are dry. Meet two students who live in desert communities. Let's follow them as they email back and forth about where they live.

Hi Aya,

Hello from the city of Tucson (TOO-sahn), Arizona! My name is Elena, and I am 9 years old. Arizona is a state in the United States that has deserts. I learned from my teacher that Siwa Oasis is a desert in the country of Egypt. Could you please tell me about where you live? I'm glad our teachers planned for us to email each other! Here's a picture of me with my dog and a picture of my house.

'Bye! Elena

Hi Elena,

I am also 9, and I'm happy to email you! What is your cute dog's name? 😊

I've attached pictures of me and my little brother, Omar, and of Siwa Oasis. An **oasis** is a surprising place. It has lots of plants and water, even though it is in the middle of a desert. Siwa Oasis is in the Sahara, a desert that covers most of my country, Egypt.

It's hot here most of the year, and we get very little rain. But it gets as cold as 48°F in winter. When it's that cold, Omar and I don't like to play outside.

Email me back! Aya

Hey Aya!

My dog's name is Thunder. We got him during a thunderstorm, so it's a good name. It rains and storms a lot here during the **monsoon** season. A monsoon is a windy, heavy rainstorm. Here in Tucson, the monsoon season starts in June and can last until September. Sometimes it feels like I'm wearing my rain boots all summer. It's pretty hot and dry the rest of the year. You can see from the picture I'm sending that you and Omar wouldn't like to play outside during the monsoon season either!

Talk to you soon! Elena

Hi Elena,

The picture you sent of the monsoon is frightening. It does not thunderstorm often in Siwa Oasis. In fact, it almost never rains here. But, on windy days, sand blows into our faces from all of the sand dunes in the desert near us. Sand dunes are mountains of sand that shift in the wind.

Sometimes we must cover our mouths with our clothes so we don't breathe in the blowing sand. You and Thunder would not like windy days here. 😮

Hope to hear back from you soon! Aya

Hello Aya,

What kinds of food do you eat in Egypt? Do you have a favorite food? Tacos are my favorite meal. They are tortillas (tor-TEE-yuhs)—a kind of flat bread—filled with spicy meat. Every Saturday night, my family gets tacos from my favorite restaurant (see my picture). I always give Thunder a little. Tacos are his favorite food, too!

You wrote that your town doesn't get much rain. So where does the water you drink come from? Most of our water comes from a river many miles away. We try not to use too much extra water here. 😋

Later! Elena

TAQUERIA

TAQUERIA

·TACOS
·TORTAS
·BURROS
·MARISCOS
·SEA FOOD

·HORCHATA
·LIMONADA
·FOUNTAIN DRINKS

Dear Elena, 😃

We get our water from **springs**. They are places where fresh water flows from deep in the ground. Springs are all over Siwa Oasis. The spring water makes our oasis beautiful by helping trees and plants grow.

The tacos in your picture look delicious. I wish Siwa Oasis had a taco restaurant so I could try them. We eat many kinds of foods in Egypt. My favorite is falafel, made of ground chickpeas patted into balls and fried. My mother makes bread to wrap around the falafel, and it looks a little like tacos. I wish I could email you some!

Here's my father at a falafel dinner. I helped mom make the dinner to celebrate Omar's football team's success. You call football "soccer" in the United States, right? Do you play a sport?

Email again soon! Aya

Hi Aya, 😊

I am sending you and Omar a picture of my softball team. I'm standing at home plate dressed in a gray and black uniform. I'm a good batter. I've hit three home runs this year so far. Last year my team won almost all of our games!

I like to take a bike ride to warm up before a game. Today, I saw three lizards while I rode my bike. A lot of lizards live in the desert. I have decided that seeing lizards before a game is a sign that my team will win.

I wonder if you play a sport, Aya.

Email me back! Elena

Dear Elena,

I don't play sports. But Omar tries to get me to play football with him and his friends from the neighborhood. They play right across the street from our house. Sometimes I walk over there to cheer my brother on. Here is a picture I have taken of one of their games. Maybe one day I will play!

We have lizards here in Siwa Oasis, too. I like watching them climb on the walls. Sometimes I try to catch one when it is sunning itself, but it always runs away!

I enjoy our emails! Aya

Check In Describe how Aya and Elena's lives are similar and different in their desert communities.

Discuss

1. What do you think connects the three selections you read in this book? What makes you think that?

2. How do saguaro and prickly pear cacti provide homes and food to living things in the desert?

3. Describe how some plants and animals are adapted to live in land as dry as the desert.

4. Would you like to live in a desert community like the ones you read about? Why or why not?

5. What do you still want to know about deserts and desert communities? How can you learn more?